S M A R T · P L

Professor Sir Ghillean Prance FRS likes to be called Iain. He was named 'Ghillean' after a mountain on the Scottish Isle of Skye where he grew up during the Second World War. He loved the wild coastline and the whole world of nature on his doorstep.

As a teenager he was sent to school in England. His biology master noticed his fascination with plants and encouraged him to go out plant hunting in the holidays. Later Iain went to Oxford University to study botany and started to go overseas on plant hunting expeditions.

His first was to Turkey with his student friends. Then he went to the Amazon river in South America. He so loved the tropical rainforest that he decided to make his career there, discovering plants. So much was still unknown in the Amazon.

For twenty-five years he led expeditions to collect plants in many unexplored areas, using rubber boats on the rivers and walking lost trails with local Indians. He found hundreds of new plants and helped conservationists save some of the rainforest by planning forest reserves with the Brazilian government.

He became Director of the Royal Botanic Gardens, Kew, just after the terrible hurricane of October 1987. There was a lot of repair work to do. Now the gardens are restored and lead the world in conservation and botanical science.

NAMING • PLANTS

TAXONOMY is the science of naming and classifying plants.

It is estimated that there are 300,000 different flowering plants in the world, of which 250,000 have been found and named, though this does not include microscopic plants.

A list of plant names (usually by country) is called a FLORA. This is very helpful when looking for plants which may give us new medicines or more useful crops.

In thirty years of plant hunting Iain has discovered over four hundred plant species new to science.

Whoever finds a new plant can name it. Plants have two names. Usually the first name, the group or GENUS, is already known. So is the plant FAMILY. It is the SPECIES, the second name, which must be chosen. Botanists do not name plants after themselves, but respected friends or scientists or a special feature on the plant itself.

First they must prove their discovery by writing down a detailed description in a special code called BOTANICAL LATIN. This is understood, and checked, internationally.

It is a great honour to have a plant named after you. Iain has had forty three! Most are called 'PRANCEI'.

1.
Where was the world's first botanical garden?
(Answer: page 25)

SMART QUIZ

ANIMAL • LINKS

What do you mean *"What's for dinner?"*

The Leaf Cutter Ant

Science has known for a long time that certain plants are vital to some animals. Koala bears can eat little but the Eucalyptus tree. Leaf Cutter ants live underground tending a single type of home-grown fungus. Indian rhinos eat river bank grasses, often just the Trewia tree.

Now we are learning that some plants cannot live without certain animals. Most people know that bees carry pollen from flower to flower and without this the plants could not breed. But some, like orchids, make this a tough job, even though only one type of bee likes them. Others need special bats, birds or furry animals to carry the pollen.

Some of the ways animals help plants are so wild and strange that they seem to be doing it just for fun. But if just one link is missed in a chain of events, the plant—and perhaps the animal—will die. Iain himself now takes up the story...

The Temperate House, Royal Botanic Gardens, Kew

2.
What plants caused a famous mutiny?
(Answer: page 25)

SMART QUIZ

THE · ROYAL WATERLILY

VICTORIA · AMAZONICA

A good example of the link with animals is the ROYAL WATERLILY.

This giant waterlily is the largest in the world. Its lily pads, up to 2.5 metres across, can hold up a baby. It grows in river backwaters and lakes in the rainforest. Its full name is VICTORIA AMAZONICA and was named after Queen Victoria by a pioneer plant hunter, Dr John Lindley, who first described it in 1836.

It was first made to flower in Kew in the 1840s. Here we pollinate it by paint brush! Gently touching the pollen from one flower to another. It wasn't until 1973 that I discovered how it happened naturally. It is a strange story...

I might have called it a beetles' all night lock-in party!

At sunset the white lily flowers create their own warmth and open to fill the air with a strong perfume. Nearby scarab beetles smell this and fly to the flowers and feed on the sugar and starch inside.

At midnight the flowers close up. The beetles, about eight at a time, are trapped inside. They go on feeding. The next day the flowers turn purple, release pollen and re-open.

The freed beetles fly off, brushing pollen onto their sticky bodies as they squeeze out. That night they smell another white flower and as they land they pollinate it.

3.
What is the quickest moving plant in the world?
(Answer: page 25)

SMART QUIZ

THE
BRAZIL · NUT
BERTHOLLETIA · EXCELSA

The BRAZIL NUT is very special to me. It is my favourite nut and I have studied it a great deal. It is found in most places in the flood-free areas of the Amazon rainforest.

It wasn't until an American scientist, Dr Scott Mori, and I researched it carefully that we realised just how lucky we are to have the Brazil Nut at all.

To start with, in parts of the forest the nut is known as a dangerous killer. The nut grows in clusters inside a very hard pod high up (60 metres) in the tree canopy. When ripe, it plunges down like a cannon ball.

If you are standing underneath it will give you a lot more than a headache! This makes collecting risky. During January and February, when the pods fall, many nut collectors avoid the forest altogether.

But how does the tree grow in the first place?

4.
How do Kew botanists save lives?
(Answer: page 25)

SMART QUIZ

We once tried planting some nuts here at Kew, which I had brought back from Brazil. But they would not grow. We tried everything—and Kew gardeners know a lot about growing unusual plants. In the end, the only thing which worked was cutting two small nicks in the shell, just as if an animal had bitten it, before planting. Then it grew right away.

This reminded us that in the forest the only animal which can eat the nut is the Agouti, which is like a large rat. Its jaws and teeth are very strong. It also buries a lot of nuts and, like the squirrel, forgets where some of them are. These grow up into the new Brazil Nut trees. Of course these nuts have bites in already—where the Agouti has carried them.

But that is not all. The nuts can only grow if the tree flower has been pollinated. And they don't make this easy.

The only insect which can do it is a large and muscular bee—bees like the bumble bee (much bigger than in England), the carpenter bee and one or two others, called EUGLOSSINE bees.

They love Brazil Nut flowers, but also orchid flowers, especially STANHOPE'S ORCHID. So Brazil Nut trees must have orchids growing nearby, or the bees will not come.

The bee lands on the flower, but cannot get at the nectar inside without forcing open a spring-loaded 'hood'. If it is strong enough to do this, the spring action of the hood forces the back of the bee against the pollen in the flower and rubs some of it off.

The bee flies on to find another flower, pushes inside, and scrapes some of its pollen onto the flower, pollinating it.

So the nut we all enjoy at Christmas needs special bees, certain orchids, a forgetful mammal and brave collectors to get on our tables. No wonder it is worth having!

Opposite page: main photo, the Brazil Nut tree. Inset: Cattleya orchid

Below left: the Agouti

Below right: two women working in a Brazil Nut factory

THE CALABASH

CRESCENTIA · CUJETE

The CALABASH is the Tupperware of the Amazon! It is a natural gourd. Fully grown it is a round, football-sized wood shell. Cut in two, it is used for everything from cups, plates and dishes to pots and pans, hard hats, canoe balers, wash bowls, garden trowels and food storage jars. But it owes its survival to one of the smallest insects —the ant, and one of the strangest mammals —the bat.

In the Amazon bats have a bad name, mainly because the famous VAMPIRE lives there. It really does drink blood, though it doesn't kill its victims.

Bat pollinating a flower.

5.
What is the oldest living plant?
(Answer: page 25)

SMART QUIZ

It nicks open a tiny wound (when the animal is asleep) and licks, very fast, for an hour or so and then leaves.

The wound will go on bleeding, as there is an anti-clotting chemical in the Vampire's bite. Sometimes an infection can set in, sickening or killing the animal.

The bat which pollinates the Calabash is not a Vampire bat but one of the many species in the rainforest where they are the most common mammal. It is called the GLOSSOPHAGA bat.

The Calabash flower is green and unattractive. But the bat cannot see. The flower sticks out from the branch, so the bat can find it with its echo locator, and smell its scent. The bat takes a drink of nectar and so brushes pollen onto its head. This is carried on to the next flower.

As the fruit starts growing, it is small, green and soft like a large apple. Ideal food for the birds and animals of the rainforest. So why is it not stripped from the trees? Well, it develops small pimples, or nectaries, on its smooth skin. These are very sweet and attract a fierce ant which loves the honey taste.

The ants are very jealous and anything, no matter how large, which takes a fancy to the fruit is attacked by the angry tenants. It quickly loses interest.

When the Calabash is fully grown, it turns brown. Now it is tough and woody and is no longer tasty. The animals leave it alone. The nectaries and the ants disappear, leaving it to be cut down and used by the people of the Amazon.

The Calabash in use

GUARANA

PAULLINIA • CUPANA

GUARANA is the coca-cola of the Amazon. It is very popular and sold in bottles. It packs quite a punch, having five times more caffeine than coffee! It tastes a bit like fizzy apple juice and is really refreshing in the warm climate.

It is a very pretty plant, though strange to look at. Like a stalk with a lot of eyeballs tied onto it!

Fruit loving birds spot the red rimmed 'eyes' and they stop to feed on the soft white flesh, swallowing the darker seeds. They leave the seeds in their droppings, perhaps many miles away, where they grow up into new plants.

Guarana is pollinated by small bees in the common way, but it will defend itself like the Calabash by attracting fierce ants with large nectar pools on its young leaves.

6.
What is the world's largest plant?
(Answer: page 25)

SMART QUIZ

GUARANÁ
Amazonas

ORCHIDS

ORCHIDS are some of the world's most beautiful flowers. But like many beauties they ask much from those who serve them.

Bulbophyllum macranthum

7.
What are 'air plants'?
(Answer: page 25)

SMART QUIZ

One of the worst is the BUCKET ORCHID. It produces a liquid scent in its petal 'bucket'. This is picked up by male bees in the forest and, knowing they will need oil from the orchid to attract a mate, they crowd around to collect it. Soon one slips into the bucket.

The only way out, as the sides of the bucket are wet and slippery, is through a narrow petal tunnel. As the bee struggles through, he collects a dollop of pollen on his back. If he goes swimming in another bucket, he must get out again by the tunnel, where his pollen ball is neatly hooked off on a tiny spike. Hard luck for him, but good for the orchid!

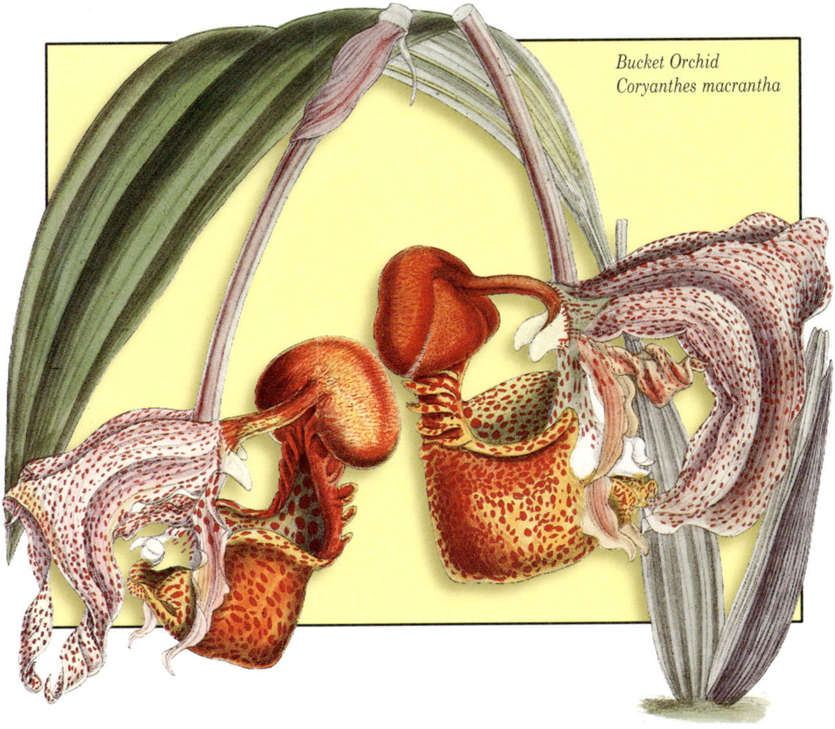

Bucket Orchid
Coryanthes macrantha

BEE • ORCHID

OPHRYS • APIFERA

Some orchids attract bees by playing the great pretender.

The BEE ORCHID looks just like a female bee. A passing male even smells the same exciting scent. He zooms down in a mating position and his weight tips the top of the flower onto his head, touching it with pollen. Disappointed, he buzzes off only to be seduced by another flower—which tips over and neatly lifts the pollen from him when he lands.

What the bee feels about this is not on record!

Other orchids make *sure* the insect does the business.

The BULBOPHYLLUM MACRANTHUM attracts flies to land on a fine ridge of petals. As they battle to hang on they trip a plant lever and are thrown up against the base of the flower. Buzzing angrily at this reception, they pick up the pollen. On the next flower they are treated just the same, leaving some behind. Heads are spinning by the end of the day. But the forest is blooming!

8.
What plants grow at the N and S Poles?
(Answer: page 25)

SMART QUIZ

THE
SAND-BOX·TREE
HURA·CREPITANS

The SAND-BOX is a real wild one of the rainforest. For a start it fires its seeds out—in all directions—to make sure they are spread properly. It shoots up to 15 metres! The crackling sound of the seed pods going off has made many explorers think they have run into a gun fight!

The pod, with the seeds inside, dies and then dries in the sun. After this it begins to warp. Suddenly the dried husk will split open under the strain and catapult the seeds out into the forest. It is called the Sand-box tree because, before the days of blotting paper, the seeds were often wired together, filled with sand, and used for blotting ink.

It has a smaller English cousin called the HIMALAYAN BALSAM. Children use it in a game to see who can shoot the farthest.

But shooting is only the start. The tree produces a nasty poison to protect itself. If the Amazon Indians want to cut a Sand-box tree down they cover their eyes. They find it very difficult to cut a tree down without looking, but if they don't do this they will be blinded by the spurting sap. Their hands and arms are always sore for many days afterwards.

Only one animal can enjoy the fruit—the MACAW. This strikingly coloured forest bird munches away at the fruit from the poison tree without a care in the world, for it knows the secret antidote. After eating the Macaw flies down to a part of the river bank and pecks away some of the clay porcelain there. This neutralises the poison. Rather muddy as an after-dinner mint. But, like mint with humans, it settles the Macaw's stomach—quite safely.

The Sand-box tree
Hura crepitans

AMORPHOPHALLUS · TITANUM

TITAN ARUM

Very nearly the tallest flower in the world is the TITAN ARUM. It was first grown at Kew in 1889, from a seed given to the garden by its discoverer Odoardo Beccari. It flowers only very rarely. It has one big leaf and a massive spike covered in tiny flowers which grows over 2 metres tall.

And it stinks to high heaven! When it flowers, it heats up (just like the Royal Waterlily) and spreads a dreadful pong in the air, smelling rather like rotting meat. This is designed to attract flies so they will take away its pollen. Flies love nothing better than rotting meat, so the plant fools them long enough to pollinate itself.

When it last flowered at Kew (1996) it attracted worldwide interest, and double the usual number of visitors came to the Gardens just to see (and smell) it.

9.
How many specimens are held in Kew's Herbarium?
(Answer: page 25)

SMART QUIZ

ARISTOLOCHIA • SP

Another plant which smells awful and looks even more like rotting meat is one called ARISTOLOCHIA.

It has a trumpet shaped mouth and has inward pointing hairs to make sure the flies go in but then can't get out (like a lobster pot). They have to stay in long enough to collect a good load of pollen. After a while the hairs wilt and the flies can go free.

RAFFLESIA • SP

Rafflesia pricei

The world's largest flower is actually a parasite, growing out of a jungle creeper or vine lying on the ground (in Sumatra or Java). It is called RAFFLESIA. It is very hard to find, though it can grow to up to a metre across. Many plant hunters spend their whole lives without ever seeing it.

It isn't very pretty, with 2 cm thick cardboard-like brown petals with white blotches on. It has no leaves or stalk, but it is very impressive for all that.

It is pollinated by flies, ants, squirrels and wild pigs which go to it—also because of its strange smell.

10.
How much rainforest is lost every 6 minutes?
(Answer: page 25)

SMART QUIZ

AMAZING!

After 35 years of working in science I am still staggered by the many amazing ways which plants work with animals, and each other, to keep on growing all over the world.

The design of every relationship is so beautiful, sometimes complicated, and often quite funny.

And we cannot do without these meetings happening. Nowhere in the world can we exist without the support of plants: renewing the air we breathe (for plants give off oxygen); providing the basic food we eat, such as cereal, rice or potatoes; making up the clothes we wear like cotton and linen; or keeping us sheltered and warm with wood to burn and timber to build.

Even our hi-tech cars and planes would stop without fuel and oil—which is decayed plant fibre from ancient times.

For many years I have believed that God is the great designer behind all nature. I have been a firm Christian since my days as a botany student in Oxford, when I first heard the life of Christ explained clearly. All my studies in science since then have confirmed my faith. I believe there IS a great creative mind behind everything I can see through my laboratory microscope, or my binoculars in the rainforest.

To me, it's too clever to be accidental. Or, put another way, the kind of accidents I come across don't produce such wonderful results! And I don't believe God is against scientific thinking about our world. Science is a very good way to think, though not the only way. In fact I believe God wants us to think MORE about the world, not less.

For I believe the world is in great danger.

I can see it beginning to die. We are losing many types of plants and animals, our air and water are getting worse and the temperature is rising.

If this goes on happening WE will start to die too. We are part of the system, and cannot help it. This is the way it works. We will not have any choice—IF things go on the way they are.

But we CAN choose to do something before it gets too late.

To be concerned about the world we must think GLOBALLY, but to do something we must act LOCALLY.

Cocoa Yam: *Xanthosoma sagittifolia*

ACTION LIST

Here are some things I do:

- Walk, cycle or use public transport instead of a car.
- Switch off anything not needed right away (lights, TV, car)
- Avoid highly processed food.
- Repair and re-wear clothes and shoes.
- Collect waste paper at work for re-cycling and re-use.
- Use bottle & can banks to re-cycle glass, metal & plastic.
- Buy genuine 'green' products.
- Support my local Agenda 21 group.
- Use a 'wormery' to turn organic kitchen waste into compost. (A 'wormery' is a bin full of hungry worms, which eat up kitchen left-overs, turning it back into good plant food.)

Why don't you try some of these things? They really do help and save money! You can find out about Agenda 21 at your local library.

SMART QUIZ

11. How many pairs of shoes are thrown away each year? *(Answer: page 25)*

MILLENNIUM SEED • BANK PROJECT

In the year 2000 we want to open our new Millennium Seed Bank, Kew.

We already have a Seed Bank, at Wakehurst Place in Sussex, which holds many millions of seeds from all over the world. Saving seeds is a good way of conserving plant species. So far we have collected about 2% of the world's flowering plants, as seeds.

But when we open our new Millennium Seed Bank, we will be able to save 10% of the world's flowering plants by 2010.

We already hold seeds of plants which now do not exist in the wild at all!

Kew has already received many gifts from companies, individuals and trusts, but help is still needed.

Top: The Seed Bank Manager.

Top inset: GLOBEFLOWER (TROLLIUS EUROPEUS) - from the Buttercup part of the Scrophulariaceae family. Endangered due to agricultural reform.

Bottom: FIELD COW-WHEAT (MELAMPYRUM ARVENSE) - from the Figwort part of the Scrophulariaceae family. Rare due to changed farming methods.

SPONSOR A • SPECIES

The public can help Kew save as many plant species as possible by sponsoring a species. The minimum donation is £15. In return, donors will receive a Certificate of Sponsorship.

If you would like to help sponsor a species, send your cheque (made payable to The Millennium Seed Bank Appeal) to: Sponsor a Species, Millennium Seed Bank Appeal, Royal Botanic Gardens Kew, Richmond, Surrey TW9 3AB.

Perhaps you could organise a sponsored event to raise support in your area.

Bee Orchid. Ophrys apifera